silly Millies
The Tooth Fairy Tells All

Written and illustrated by
Cynthia L. Copeland

That is me—the one and only tooth fairy!

The Millbrook Press
Brookfield, Connecticut

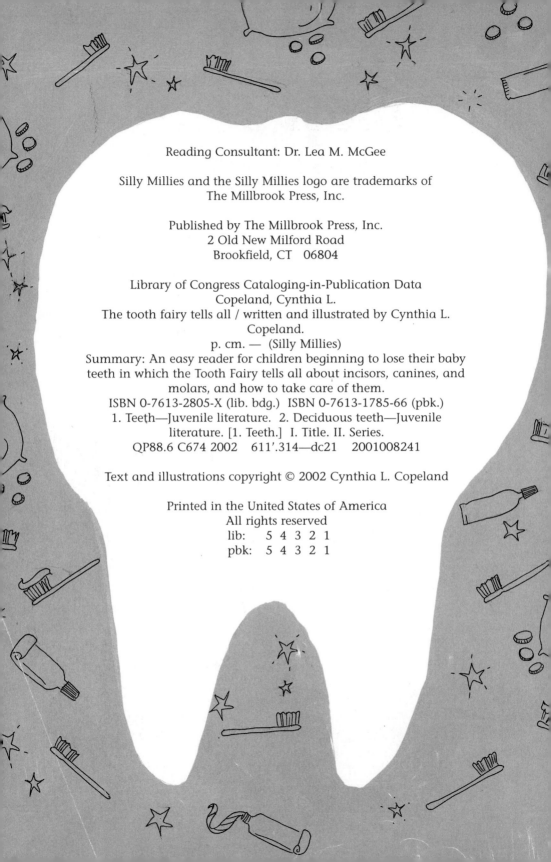

Reading Consultant: Dr. Lea M. McGee

Silly Millies and the Silly Millies logo are trademarks of
The Millbrook Press, Inc.

Published by The Millbrook Press, Inc.
2 Old New Milford Road
Brookfield, CT   06804

Library of Congress Cataloging-in-Publication Data
Copeland, Cynthia L.
The tooth fairy tells all / written and illustrated by Cynthia L.
Copeland.
p. cm. — (Silly Millies)
Summary: An easy reader for children beginning to lose their baby
teeth in which the Tooth Fairy tells all about incisors, canines, and
molars, and how to take care of them.
ISBN 0-7613-2805-X (lib. bdg.) ISBN 0-7613-1785-66 (pbk.)
1. Teeth—Juvenile literature. 2. Deciduous teeth—Juvenile
literature. [1. Teeth.] I. Title. II. Series.
QP88.6 C674 2002   611'.314—dc21   2001008241

The Tooth Fairy Tells All

4

8

13

When you are five or six years old,
your baby teeth start to wiggle.
Then they fall out, but not all at the
same time!

There are some baby teeth you will have until you are twelve years old.

If you were a shark, each tooth would only last about a week!

9/22

9/23

9/20

(The shark tooth fairy is all pooped out!)

16

17

19

22

The teeth in the middle hold and rip food.
The back teeth grind and chew food.

23

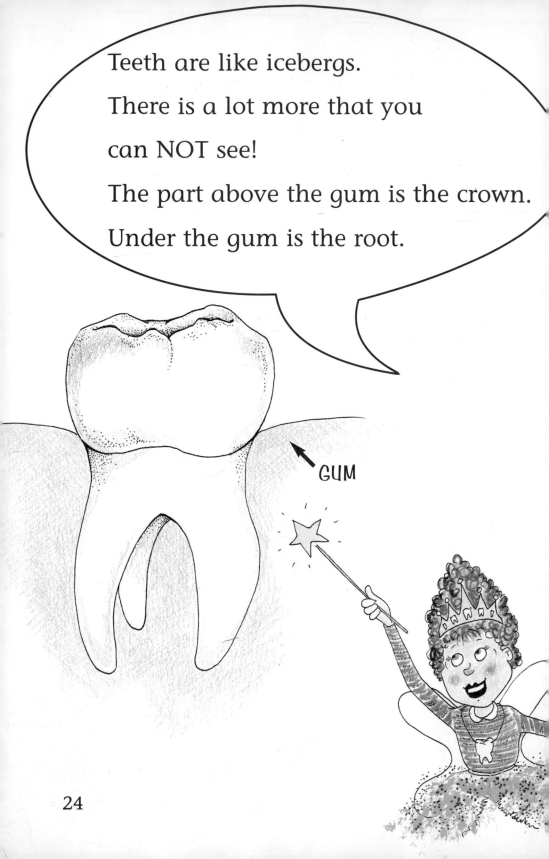

Teeth are like icebergs.
There is a lot more that you
can NOT see!
The part above the gum is the crown.
Under the gum is the root.

GUM

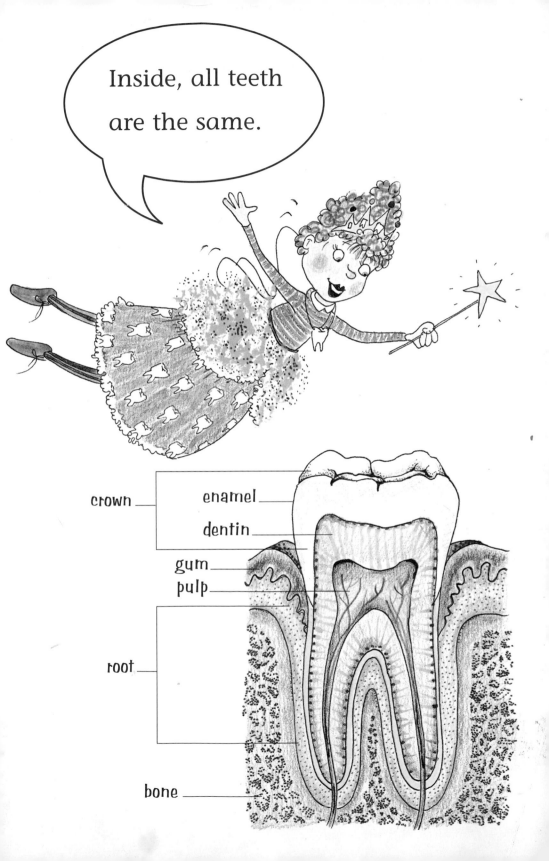

Did you know ...?

Your teeth are like your finger-prints—they are not the same as anybody else's.

In Mexico, children who lose a tooth are not visited by the Tooth Fairy. The Tooth Mouse comes to get the teeth children leave under their pillows.

A snail has 25,000 teeth—on its tongue!

Elephant tusks are really teeth.

The teeth of a lobster are in its stomach.

If you are right-handed, you probably chew with the teeth on the right side of your mouth. Left-handed people chew with the teeth on the left side of their mouth.

In the year 200 A.D., Romans used toothpaste made of eggshells, seashells, bones, and honey.

Dear Parents:

Congratulations! By sharing this book with your child, you are taking an important step in helping him or her become a good reader. *The Tooth Fairy Tells All* is perfect for children who are beginning to read alone, either silently or aloud. Below are some ideas for making sure your child's reading experience is a positive one.

Tips for Reading
- First, read the book aloud to your child. Then, if your child is able to "sound out" the words, invite him or her to read to you. If your child is unsure about a word you can help by asking, "What word do you think it might be?" or, "Does that make sense?" Point to the first letter or two of the word and ask your child to make that sound. If she or he is stumped, read the word slowly, pointing to each letter as you sound it out. Always provide lots of praise for the hard work your child is doing.
- If your child knows the words but is having trouble reading aloud, cut a plain white ruler-sized strip of paper to place under the line as your child reads. This will help your child keep track of his or her place.
- If your child is a beginning reader, have her or him read this book aloud to you. Reading and rereading is the best way to help any child become a successful reader.

Tips for Discussion
- The Tooth Fairy looks silly hiding Easter eggs and pretending to be Santa Claus. Who else could the Tooth Fairy pretend to be?
- In this book the reader gets to know the characters of the Tooth Fairy and Wisdom Tooth. How are they alike? Different?
- Can the reader predict what Wisdom Tooth will do now that he is out of the tooth business?

Lea M. McGee, Ed.D.
Professor, Literacy Education
University of Alabama